GOOD BOY JESSE

The story of a dog named Jesse, as narrated by himself

GOOD BOY JESSE

The story of a dog named Jesse, as narrated by himself

Written by

Roberta R. Chadis

To Kim —
Always follow your dreams.
Love,
Roberta
4/14/2014

BEST BILINGUAL SOLUTIONS
A Publishing House for the Citizen of the World™
Cambridge, Massachusetts, U.S.A.

Copyright © 2011 by Best Bilingual Solutions, Inc.
No part of this publication may be reproduced, stored in a retrieval system, or transmitted in any form or by any means, electronic, photocopying, scanning, or otherwise, without the prior written permission of the Publisher. Exceptions are made explicitly for brief passages used in printed and web-based reviews and articles.

Published by
Best Bilingual Solutions, Inc.
One Broadway, 14th Floor
Cambridge, MA 02142 U.S.A.
www.BestBilingual.com

ISBN-10: 1-61995-459-1
ISBN-13: 978-1-61995-459-5

Printed in the United States of America
2 3 4 5 6 7 8 9 10   BBS1   18 17 16 15 14 13
First English Edition: December 2011

Please note that this book is also being published bilingually, in many pairs of languages. Please visit our website at *BestBilingual.com* to purchase physical and downloadable bilingual editions, and to participate in discussions and forums related to this book.

This book is available at quantity discounts for bulk purchases. For information, please call 1-888-324-5494, or email us at *bookstore@bestbilingual.com*.

CONTENTS

Acknowledgments		*vii*
Preface		*ix*
Dedication		*xiii*
1.	"Good Boy, Jesse"	1
2.	Home	5
3.	Stairs	7
4.	It's a Dog's Life	10
5.	Follow Me	14
6.	Jesse's Song	15
7.	Music To My Ears	16
8.	Breakfast	18
9.	Walks	23
10.	Does He Bite?	26
11.	Mom and Dad	27
12.	OK	30
13.	Vacation	31
14.	Jesse's Dog Resume	33
15.	"P" is for Personality, Piddles, and Poops	36
16.	School	41
17.	The *Good Boy Jesse* Alphabet	43
18.	Dog Beautiful	46
19.	Christmas	48
20.	Happiness Is	52
21.	Epilogue: Mom Speaks	54
22.	Epilogue: Dad Speaks	56
23.	Tribute	58
24.	Dreams	60
25.	From the Author	63

Acknowledgments

Whenever you take on a project there are people who help you in ways you cannot imagine. You share your idea and get encouragement, inspiration and enthusiasm for your passionate efforts to publish a book. To all of my relatives, friends and strangers in my path, much thanks for your support.

I am indebted to my dear and trusted friends who read my book first: Lajla LeBlanc, Fiona Barrett, Donald Hunter, Ruth Estrich, Matt Caruso, and several others who gave their time and energy to proofread, suggest improvements and simply be cheerleaders for "Good Boy Jesse."

The other human who has my heartfelt appreciation is my publisher and friend, Julian G. Franco, from Best Bilingual Solutions, Inc., who turned a personal coffee table book into a worthwhile endeavor, with unending possibilities in the bilingual world, for young and old to learn a new language.

But most of all, my lifelong thanks go to my dog, my Good Boy Jesse, who with his soulful brown eyes and heart of gold continues to live in spirit through this, his book.

PREFACE

In 1994, I wrote a story about my precious Golden, Jesse. We spent many years together as two kindred spirits and he became a source of constant joy and companionship.

Jesse seemed to possess an intelligence that transcended the normal dog persona and I began to wonder how he thought about his life and how he might tell me what he was thinking. Through Jesse's loving eyes and body language, I am certain that I have captured his unspoken description of his feelings and perceptions as *Good Boy Jesse*.

Imagine what it is like to be a Golden Retriever as you settle into a comfortable chair to read this book. Just think about the possibilities of running on the beach with the wind in your face chasing a green tennis ball; catching it in your mouth and then dropping it on the sand.

I can sense that you are smiling now and may even be waiting for me to throw the ball across the water so you can swim out to grab it and bring it back; hoping to play this game over and over. This is the nature of a Golden, like that of a child who is carefree and easily entertained with the simple things of life.

When you finish reading this page, close your eyes again and picture how it would feel to have four legs and an innocent love of adventure. After you have opened your eyes and you are human again, pretend that Jesse is close by your side and start reading.

If you concentrate very hard on each word, you may even hear the low rumble in his throat as he shares his life with you. You can close your eyes now, but don't fall asleep until you read all about *Good Boy Jesse*.

Jesse and Mom

My book is dedicated to,

♥ Mom for her inspiration, sensitivity and total devotion.

♥ Dad, for his love and discipline.

You are my family!

With unconditional love,

Good Boy Jesse

"GOOD BOY, JESSE"

Ever since I can remember, Mom and Dad have been saying, *Good Boy Jesse*. They smile at me, pat my head, look in my eyes and I know all is well.

There is something about eye contact that goes way beyond barking. It is that twinkle of light in human eyes that makes me feel all warm inside. That twinkle is hard to find in Dad's eyes because he is so darn serious and strict with me all the time. With Mom, it is a whole different story because the expression on her face always gives her away.

Mom does not know how sweet she is when she talks to me. I wonder if she caught on to the secret that I understand her completely. At least she doesn't treat me like any ordinary dog in the street!

As you can already tell, I am not ordinary, and I feel fortunate to have such a nurturing Mom and Dad who make me feel loved. Golden Retrievers have a reputation for being lovable and smart, you know, and I happen to be exceptional in the smart category. At least that is what I keep hearing. I have heard it so often I believe it; wouldn't you?

So, I decided to write this book to tell everyone about my life with Mom and Dad. If you heard some of the things Mom and Dad say, you would want to write a book too!

Dad is always saying things like, "I wonder what Jesse is thinking about in that little dog brain of his?", and he often asks Mom, "What do you think Jesse does when he is alone in the house all day?"

Mom thinks she has all the right answers to Dad's questions about what I am thinking. Maybe she should just come right out and ask me? Sometimes she is right; sometimes she is dead wrong; and sometimes I just want to tell her that she is giving me way too much credit. After all, I am only a dog, right?

Now, I know what you are thinking. You think I asked Mom and Dad to write this book for me, but that would be impossible! They are much too busy to do something as silly as write down what I have to say.

Can you see Mr. Serious sitting at his desk taking dictation from a dog? Mom, on the other paw, is too busy reading her mail and talking into a bone-shaped object that she holds next to her ear when she gets home from work. She hardly has the energy to brush me before I go to sleep.

At least they have time to tell me how good I am, and a little too much time to tell me I am a bad dog when I eat my toys and chew on towels! Boy, do I love to chew towels...

Back to the issue of who is writing this book — it is me, *Good Boy Jesse*. After all, I have nothing else to do all day long other than thinking, listening, house-sitting and sleeping. Just thinking about sleeping has given me the urge to take a short catlike nap, and when I wake up I will tell you all about me, *Good Boy Jesse*.

By the way, my real name is *Jesse*. Mom and Dad chose the name "Jesse" because it was as close as they could get to Dad's favorite name "Jessica" and it was too late to trade me in. Boy am I lucky! A very lucky dog!

I was once a puppy too!

HOME

My first day with Mom was an experience for both of us. I was not thrilled about leaving my brothers and sisters and I did not like the looks of the collar and leash.

I was also confused because I did not see Dad! Mom's welcome hug was the sign I needed and I knew she was glad to see me and I hoped for the best. Since I needed her to like me, I acted as happy as a puppy could act.

I can tell you now that I won her over at the start in about an hour; the hour it took to drive to my new home. Mom and I were a team. She drove the car and I drove her crazy.

All I wanted was a little attention. You know how puppies can be. We like to be where the action is, and sitting in Mom's lap with one paw on the steering wheel seemed perfect to me! Mom thought I just wanted to be close to her, so it was love at first sight.

That first day was quite exciting. I rode in Mom's car, saw my new home, went to the veterinarian and slept all alone in my special house that Dad built for me. That special house was really a secured area to keep me out of trouble.

I literally grew up in the kitchen for the first year of my life and I am a better dog for it! My crate was my favorite place to sleep and gather my thoughts. I had all my toys and blankets in my crate and no one could hurt me in the safety of this metal home in the kitchen.

Mom and Dad had further protected me by putting two gates across the doorways to the kitchen. There was no way that anyone could harm *Good Boy Jesse*!

Speaking of Good Boy Jesse... it's time that I explain how I adopted this nickname. No lengthy commentary is required because it is obvious that I am simply an amazing animal.

I have all the right physical attributes and I am as smart as a whip. I know when to behave and when to be mischievous. I know exactly when to be what Mom and Dad call a "Good Boy." I've got it mastered and I'm proud to bark out loud about it... So that is how I got the expanded name of *Good Boy Jesse*. I am truly a good dog. Get it?

STAIRS

Before we take another step, I would like to talk a little about stairs. First, I would love to meet the person who invented them and ask why they didn't consult with me on the design. I think an escalator is much easier, of course.

The fact is that dogs have four legs. Should I start with my left front paw, my right front paw, or just use both of them and pounce like a rabbit? The answer is to simply walk up those stairs one step at a time. I have been practicing every day for almost three years and have become a professional stair climber.

The challenge is going down. You try it! First, get down on your hands and knees. Just looking down the stairs could make you change your mind and you will stay right where you are.

If you are as courageous as I am, you would take a deep breath, lift your hands off the floor and walk down those stairs like an expert. When you reach the landing you will quickly agree that dogs deserve an Olympic gold medal for stair walking.

I admit I was not picture perfect the first time I tried. The rhythm is tricky, the timing is critical, and my tail gets me in trouble.

Mom and Dad have quite a laugh watching me. They think I look like a rocking horse bouncing down the stairs. This is quite humbling for *Good Boy Jesse*, the practically perfect dog.

As I mentioned, stairs used to be difficult

IT'S A DOG'S LIFE

How many times have you heard people say they would like to come back in their next life as a dog. They think it is easy being a dog like me. They are fed, sheltered and loved as the family pet.

From my point of view as a Golden, I cannot blame them for feeling that way. When I come back in my next life, I certainly would not want to come back as a person! A dog's life has real meaning and structure. Mom and Dad depend on me for love and devotion.

I know they would miss my handsome furry face and the wag of my tail. They would never have as much fun staying at home if I weren't in their way all the time.

Dogs inherently know how to be who they are. There are no books in the library that give instructions to puppies on the best behavior traits of animals and how to develop your skills as a dog!

So how did I learn what to do and what not to do? You guessed it. I had to learn from Mom and Dad.

They did all the reading about animal behavior and development and enrolled me in "Puppy School" where I showed all the other pups what to do.

Behaving like a dog comes natural, but learning the difference between right and wrong is taught using treats, commands, body language and patience.

At school, I was always getting in trouble because I did not listen or have the best discipline. Yes, I pulled my head out of my collar and would not stay in the "SIT" position until told "OK" to move. I just could not understand why I had to be so obedient all the time.

Why did I need to go to school anyway? I have a great sense of smell and hearing that you cannot learn from any teacher. My keen animal insight is proven by my ability to know when things are wrong by the sound of people's voices and the cadence of their walk.

I'm on my best paw with other dogs in the street and people that I meet, after all, with a name like *Good Boy Jesse*, what would you expect?

It was after I graduated that I started applying what I learned at school in real life; like waiting at the curb for cars to pass before I crossed the street.

Mom and Dad, by the way, graduated with honors and told all their friends that I was the best dog in the whole class.

If you think it's easy being a dog, think again. It's the hardest thing in the world if you do not understand human behavior. When Mom and Dad are talking loudly, I know it is time for a nap in a quiet corner.

At dinner time, we all gather in the dining room and I settle in under the table waiting for treats. You must be able to read lips and understand a foreign language almost from birth.

I wonder if people realize how much a dog thinks about all day long. After all, it's a dog's life.

Here I am waiting to go out

FOLLOW ME

Mom and Dad bless the day they brought me home because along with the joy of raising me they also got a constant companion.

I do not know how I learned it, but I have been following Mom and Dad around the house since the day I moved in. Wherever they go, I go. Wherever they sit, I sit. Wherever they stand, I stand. Wherever they sleep, I sleep. Wherever they eat, I look on with anticipation of a falling crumb.

Whenever they look up, I look up. If they stop, I stop. If they move, I move. If they go upstairs, I go upstairs. If they go downstairs, I go downstairs. If they are sad, I'm quiet. When they are happy, I am full of the devil. When they are hugging each other, I am right there in the middle. We are inseparable!

I am not sure who needs whom more, them or me. We will go on like this forever. They are my leaders and I am their faithful follower. Follow me!

Now you can follow me into my home where I spent my time listening to music. One day, Mom got inspired and wrote a song about me.

Jesse's Song

Come lay by my side, Jesse dear.
Come stay with me for a while.
We can stare at the sea and smell the salt air,
Let me feel your warm body next to mine.

Shall I tell you a story of squirrels and birds?
Do you know where the ducks sleep at night?
Let's run on the sand and discover a treasure
That waits for us like an angel in the light.

Come lay by my side, Jesse dear.
Come stay with me for a while.
We can stare at the sea and smell the salt air,
Let me feel your warm body next to mine.

Let's walk side by side, Jesse Boy.
Your sweet soul has touched my heart.
We'll hug the wind in silence,
You and me, Jesse Boy.
It was love at first sight from the start.

Come lay by my side, Jesse dear.
Come stay with me for a while.
We can stare at the sea and smell the salt air,
Let me feel your warm body next to mine.

MUSIC TO MY EARS

You and I know that dogs have extremely good hearing and excellent taste. You also know that classical music has been referred to as longhair music. If you put a longhair Golden Retriever like me in a room with a quality sound system, you can be sure to have a perfectly orchestrated ensemble right before your eyes.

Thanks to Dad, I have been listening to classical music all my life and I have learned that "You become what you hear." There are variations on this theme and I would like to share mine with you.

When I hear Mozart, Bach and Vivaldi, I feel at peace with the world. The classics keep me company all day. It is very soothing to the soul to hear the violins, trumpets and bassoons vibrating through the house.

Sometimes I like to sit with Mom and Dad and listen to the sounds as they change in volume and speed. The louder and faster it gets, the more excited I feel. If the melody is slow, I daydream. I wonder if that is the way Mom and Dad feel.

There also seem to be people in the house when the music changes to conversation. I cannot figure out where they are. It sounds like they are in the room, but I just can't see them. I will figure it out, but for now I will just sit pretty and tune in to the next piece.

I might even take a quick nap. You know, I cannot even imagine what I would be like if Mom and Dad listened to rock and roll or hard rock music. How I could I sleep? How does anyone relax when the music is so loud and the instruments are electronic?

I am sure I would not be the calm individual that I am today. Life revolves around your environment and what you were born with; again I got lucky! There is no doubt in my mind that I resonated more with classical music.

So remember my philosophy when you bring your new puppy home and you will have a well-balanced and tuned in dog just like *Good Boy Jesse*. In a world without the spoken word, good music is a feast for any dog's ears.

It's time for breakfast; are you hungry?

BREAKFAST

Daylight is breaking and I'm ready to start another day. I get up, stretch my legs and breathe on Dad until he gets the hint that it's time to get up for breakfast.

One of his eyes opens and we have dog/Dad eye contact. No words are spoken. It is that understanding between a dog and his Dad, if you know what I mean!

I have this daily schedule down to a science of sounds and actions. Let me give you an example of breakfast in the life of *Good Boy Jesse*.

It's a waiting game. I wait for sounds of life in the bedroom like a cat waiting for a mouse to leave its hole. As soon as Mom or Dad has moved an eyelid, I am ready for the morning to begin.

I always wake up happy and hungry, too. But patience is one of my better virtues and I have learned that I must wait until the stage is set properly before I can have breakfast.

I never know if Mom will feed me or I have to wait for Dad to get up, so I have developed a keen sense of what is going to happen by the pattern of events.

If Mom gets up first and goes downstairs to the kitchen before Dad, then I know that she will take me out for a piddle and that is all! I can tell because she totally ignores me and makes breakfast for herself.

A dog can perceive things very clearly by body language and expressions on faces; especially on the faces of Mom and Dad. So, when Mom ignores me, I go right back upstairs and wait for signs of life from Dad.

I think he waits for Mom to finish her breakfast and get in the shower before he decides to get up. We can both smell the coffee and the next seating for breakfast begins with Dad and his dog.

We leave Mom in the bathroom and bounce downstairs to the kitchen and I stand right in front of my bowls and give Dad "The Look".

He says something like, "I know, Jesse, you want breakfast, don't you?" and he pours fresh water in my dish.

These dishes are special, too, of course. My food dish is on the left and has the words "Good Boy" printed in black with little brown bones along with balls and paw prints. My water dish is on the right and has the word "Jesse" printed in black on the little brown bones with balls and paw prints, too.

Now, I bet you cannot guess who bought them for me. That's right, it was Dad. He had to have the best bowls for his best canine friend.

By now, I'm really hungry and I follow Dad into the room where my food is kept. He scoops out a cup of food, adds a vitamin and some brewer's yeast and garlic pills (yum) and we go back into the kitchen again.

I am now salivating (a nice way to say that I am drooling) and I am begging for my breakfast by sitting up and looking adorable. I wait for Dad to say, "OK" after we have meaningful eye contact and I bolt for my breakfast. It's gone in exactly sixty-seconds and now I want cup #2, which is sitting on the counter.

I always jump up and put my paws on the counter and Dad and I bark to each other gradually raising the pitch of the bark to a soft high pitched squeak.

The food is poured in my bowl and we look at each other one more time and pretend we are growling. At last Dad says, "OK" and the food is gone in a flash. I wash it all down with a bowl of water and then play with my favorite toy of the day.

Boring for some, you might say, but not for *Good Boy Jesse*. It gives me the strength to start the day on the right paw.

Breakfast takes much longer when Mom is the waitress. She is much more entertaining than Dad. She sings to me and tells me what she is doing every step of the way and builds up to a crescendo when she finally pours the food in my bowl.

It takes a little longer, but I still get the food in the end. It's like a dance. I follow Mom and Dad around the kitchen with my eyes and my ears. I never know what they are going to do, so I need to be alert every second.

We do this routine again at the end of the day and it's called "supper." Mealtime is such a great time for all three of us to bond.

I love to crawl under the table and listen to Mom and Dad talk about their day. Believe it or not, it relaxes me so much that I fall asleep. Don't get the wrong idea, though, it is not because I am bored or anything like that. It's because Mom and Dad's voices are like music to my ears. It is like a lullaby that makes me feel calm and cozy; snug as a bug in a rug; let's just call it love.

And so we have breakfast in the morning, followed by supper in the evening and I am a happy guy throughout the whole day because of all the love that goes into each meal. Let's eat!

WALKS

What would Mom and Dad do without me? They would never leave the house in the rain and cold weather.

I feel good about our walks since it gives Mom and Dad a chance to talk, sing, yell and breathe in the fresh air. Not to mention that I have a chance to run around in the great outdoors; sniff for things I lost in the snow; chase seagulls, pigeons and squirrels, and listen to birds.

You should come along with us. You would hear Mom singing and giggling, and you would hear Dad complaining about how cold his hands are even with his gloves on. You would hear all about this place we call *The View* and all the people and houses we see along the way.

This view is a cove that extends to the ocean. At low tide, there is no water in the cove, but we love to stare out to the water.

Mom and Dad act quite different outside. They talk very loud (Dad talks loud in the house, too!) and they laugh and seem to have a great time.

They play with me and make sure I stay on the sidewalk for safety from cars.

They tell each other how lucky they are to have *Good Boy Jesse* and that their lives would not be the same without me.

Mom and Dad would never go for walks without me, so walks are very important. It makes us feel like we are a family. We can solve all the problems of the world on a good long walk by the beach.

As for me; I find sticks, smell the air and get the exercise I need to be a healthy dog. We are all much better off and I don't mind taking all the credit since I deserve it.

Enjoying the Outdoors

DOES HE BITE?

People often look at Mom and Dad when we are all out for a walk and ask, "Does he bite?"

They want to pat me, but they are very shy. Now, I know I'm a big guy and I have very large, scary white teeth, but I am a pussycat in disguise!

I would not even hurt a fly, intentionally. I cannot help it if I weigh eighty pounds soaking wet and could knock you over if I lean hard enough. I am only being affectionate.

So, my advice to strangers when you see a dog you don't know, is to always ask, "Does he bite?" because you can't always judge a dog by his looks. Not every dog is a marshmallow like me!

MOM AND DAD

It would be very hard to write a book without at least one chapter dedicated to Mom and Dad.

"Where would *Good Boy Jesse* be without *Good Old Mom and Dad*?

I would not have a very good life. Oh sure, I could find another home to live in, but it would not be quite the same. They treat me so special; just like they were my real canine Mom and Dad.

We have our daily routines and we are used to each other now. Mom and Dad are always concerned if I seem a little sad or quiet, even though I try not to complain too much when I'm bored.

They always feed me when I'm hungry. They buy me all the toys any dog could ever dream of having, and they tell me over and over that I am the best dog in the whole world.

They watch out for my safety when I'm not paying attention in the street and the park. They talk to me like I am a real human being and they make sure I am listening when they are teaching me to obey them.

They tell me all their secrets and they know I will never tell a soul! They let me chew on bones and sticks and balls.

They take me for rides and they play with me in the snow and the backyard. They even roll around with me on the rug in their bedroom. They make me feel loved, safe and very important! I get a big lump in my throat sometimes when we are all together. We look at each other and there is an unspoken and indescribable understanding between us.

So, just for the record, Mom and Dad, I think you are the greatest.

Now, don't let it go to your heads, OK?

Playing with my toys in my favorite spots

OK

I can't do anything unless Mom or Dad says it's OK.

I can't eat breakfast. I can't eat supper. I can't go outside.

I can't go inside. I can't go upstairs. I can't go downstairs.

I can't get in the car. I can't get out of the car. I can't get up. I can't sit down.

I can't move if told to stay. I can't jump on the bed. I can't bark.

I can't leave the kitchen when Mom & Dad have guests. I can't cross the street.

I can't run on the beach. I can't run in the backyard. I can't play with other dogs.

I can't chase squirrels. I can't chase cats. I can't have treats. I can't pick up sticks.

I can't eat grass. I can't eat pasta.

But... when I hear the magic word, "OK," guess what happens?

I can do anything I want. Isn't that the way it should be?

VACATION

The big question is, "Who is on vacation?" It is not me because I am too busy watching Mom and Dad and I am still at home. If what I have heard about vacations is really true, then Mom and Dad are definitely not on vacation either!

Vacations are supposed to be restful; time taken off from work to enjoy yourself and do things that are relaxing.

My idea of a vacation would be sitting around in the sun and looking for sticks or just running on the beach and swimming in the ocean. But, this was not enough for Mom and Dad!

They had to make the most of every free moment. They were up very early making breakfast every day before I even knew they were out of the bedroom.

They went to museums, movies and flea markets. They made little box lunches to take with them on day trips and cooked supper every night.

They even managed to give me a cold shower in the backyard just because I rolled around in some dirt.

Now, I ask you, "Is this a vacation?" They even let me get in bed with them for a few minutes just to see if I would behave myself. I know they feel guilty leaving me alone all day when they are at work, but I really do not mind being alone.

Everyone needs a little private time, don't you think? In retrospect, at least they spent some quality time with me while they were on vacation; I really cannot complain about that.

Looking back at this vacation, I will tell you that we were all very tired, nobody slept through the night, we all kept tripping over each other, and I, for one, was glad when Mom and Dad both went back to work.

Sorry, Mom and Dad, I hope I didn't hurt your feelings!

JESSE'S DOG RESUME

Strengths and Experience:

Good licker, Quiet, Noisy, Soft, Cuddly, Clean, Furry, Cute, Strong, Docile, Handsome, Warm, Lovable, Happy, Serious, Kind, Generous, Thoughtful, Smart, Talented, Clown, Party Animal, Protector, Pain in the Neck, Charming, Flexible, Professional Napper, Good Listener, Good Friend, Good Companion, Great Dog Personality, Appreciates Good Music, Tolerates Bad Music, Likes Cartoons & Animal Shows on TV, Inquisitive, Persistent, Neat Dresser, Excellent Sniffer, Good Paw/Eye Coordination, Considerate, Patient, Caring, Loving, Funny, Always Hungry & Thirsty, Good Swimmer, Good Runner, Good Ball Player, Good Retriever, Good Sense of Humor, Good Football Player, Watchdog, Baby Sitter, Nurse, Good Sleeper, Compassionate, Forgiving, Loves to Play, Loves Snow, Loves Rides in the Car, Loves Walks, Loves Toys & Loves Mom & Dad.

Fears:

Lightning and Thunderstorms

Education:

Post Graduate Degree, Dog Obedience School

References:

Everyone who knows Jesse.

Skills:

It really doesn't matter as long as you love dogs.

Salary Required:

Daily Doses of Love, Attention, Meals, Grooming, Bandannas, Toys, Water, Treats, Shelter, Hugs, Kisses & Unconditional Pats on the head for being a good dog.

Enjoying my backyard

"P" IS FOR PERSONALITY, PIDDLES AND POOPS

For a dog like me, those three things are what life is all about. There are only two exceptions; meals and toys!

It is not hard for me to admit that I have the best doggone personality in the world. Mom and Dad are constantly telling each other that they think I am the smartest and best looking dog they have ever seen in their lives.

Do you think they have been influenced by me? I mean, just because they are my parents, they might be giving me a little more credit than the dog next door. I try to keep up the image, however, and make everyone smile because I am such a natural at being an adorable dog.

For example, I do this great trick with my ball by rolling it around under my paw. Another thing I do is sit back on my hind legs and lift both front paws way up high. I have such a great sense of balance, that I can hold that pose for at least five seconds!

I have also mastered this look that makes Mom and Dad wonder what I am thinking about and they usually give me a great big hug and tell me they love me. I can even be humble once in a while, which is quite a nice trait for a dog.

Did I forget to mention my toys? Well, they are one of the most important things on any dog's list.

The exceptions are the ones that squeak. Who decided that dogs like these noisy devices inside of their toys? The only reason we play with them is to find the source of the squeak and kill it. It only looks like we're having a good time.

Mom and Dad think I am happy when I have a toy in my mouth and they are right!

I've even noticed that my personality has taken on some human traits from imitating Mom and Dad. Parents are definitely the best teachers in the world.

I learned how to smile by opening my mouth and showing my teeth. I can hug, dance and hop on my hind legs just like Mom and Dad. I give good licks and kisses and can shake paws at a second's notice.

I speak when spoken to; I stop when I am told; I wait at curbs before crossing the street; I check on Mom and Dad when we go for walks and make sure they don't get lost or fall behind; I act like an alarm clock every morning and make certain that Mom and Dad are on time for work; I honestly can't think of anything I do that would not make any dog lover smile —and I never exaggerate!

If this doesn't help you understand how adorable, lovable and smart I am, please send a letter with any questions to: *Good Boy Jesse*, c/o Mom and Dad, or call me Toll Free, 1-800-HI-JESSE.

My dog personality has made a major difference in our family. There is so much hugging and kissing going on that I cannot stand it. Then there's the tickling. Doesn't Mom know that dogs are not ticklish under their paws?

What about Dad? He is trying to scare me with his hair dryer. I don't quite understand what to do, but it is fun. So, dogs are great to have around. They make you smile and they pull at your heart. They can drive you crazy, but they are great company. You can say the same things about Mom and Dad.

Now, as far as piddles and poops are concerned; they are the necessities of any dog's life. The first thing I think about in the morning is how I can control myself until Mom or Dad takes me outside for a piddle.

I have already found out what happens if I piddle in the house, and I do not want that to happen ever again. The loud reprimanding lectures and angry looks of disbelief and disappointment were almost too much for me to bear.

Didn't they know I just could not wait! I have seen Mom and Dad rushing to the bathroom lots of times because they waited too long. But I really do want to do the right thing and I have been good ever since that awful day.

Poops are in the same category and probably don't need to be described, but I will tell you that I like my privacy when it is time to poop. I do not want to be watched or disturbed.

Mom and Dad know exactly what to do and they give me a big round of applause when I am done. Isn't that great?

They take such good care of Good Boy Jesse! So we talked about my lovable dog personality, piddles and poops and now I can tell you more about meals and toys.

My life revolves around eating, playing with balls and stuffed animals, bones, sticks, Frisbees and towels.

I am happiest when I have had my breakfast or supper and can lie around and play with all my toys. Dad gets mad at me because I take them all out of my toy box and leave them all over the house. Just recently he tried to teach me how to put my toys back in the box.

Now, Dad, do you really think I have the time to do that? You better check my dog job description and note that it doesn't say anything about putting toys away after use. It's too hard for me to remember.

Mom always puts them away for me anyways! It must be my charming personality.

SCHOOL

I miss school. It was great fun. Mom and Dad would take me for a long ride at night and I could play with lots of other dogs in a big room. It was tough, though, because we all had to work hard and listen to the teacher.

I did not know what to do at first, but I learned very fast. You probably expected me to be a quick learner, and I was better than most of the other dogs in the class, of course.

Mom and Dad still make me do my homework so that I don't forget my vocabulary words. Dad reminds me about all the money that he spent on my education.

I've learned to sit, stay, roll-over, lie down, take it, leave it, stand and even give a "High Five" with one paw at a time. Admirable tricks for a dog, don't you think?

I practice my homework every day when I am home alone so I can make Mom and Dad proud of me.

I hope Mom and Dad read this chapter carefully because I would like to go back to school and say hello to my teacher. She made me feel like I was the smartest dog in the class.

Teachers are good at that. I put together a little alphabet list of some of the words that are important to know for dogs, and I hope you can use them to teach your dog a few things. You can teach an old dog new words, you know!

The *Good Boy Jesse* Alphabet

A is for ANIMAL

B is for BONE

C is for CAT

D is for DOG

E is for EASY

F is for FUR

G is for GOOD

H is for HIGH FIVE

I is for ICE CUBES

J is for JESSE

K is for KISSES

L is for LICKS

M is for MOM

N is for NO

O is for OK

P is for PUPPY

Q is for QUIET

R is for ROLLOVER

S is for SUPPER

T is for TOYS

U is for UPSTAIRS

V is for VACUUM

W is for WALKS

X is for XYLOPHONE

Y is for YES

Z is for ZZZ's (NAPS)

Spending time with a friend in my yard

DOG BEAUTIFUL

A beautiful Golden Retriever like me would look like a bad fur day if it was not for Mom and Dad. I must admit it, because every day I end up with knots in my fur and have sore skin from too much licking.

Dad's style is a quick and painful brushing with these wiry brushes. The good thing is that it's over in about three minutes and I look totally groomed.

Mom's style is much more loving and gentle, but it takes her forever. She uses every grooming tool she has, including the flea comb! She makes sure that every hair has been brushed and every square inch of skin is checked for fleas and ticks.

I must look very handsome when she's finished because she and Dad always smile and give me an ice cube for being such a good sport.

The truth is that I really do like to be brushed because it feels good. I can't get to all those hard to reach places and Mom and Dad are very careful about my private parts.

So, if you are reading this chapter, Mom and Dad, I want to thank you personally for all the brushes. Every stroke shows me just how much I'm loved.

The other good part is that I always get nice compliments from people about how beautiful I look. So thanks again, Mom and Dad, and please try not to complain about all that vacuuming! I'm only doing my small part of the job of replacing all that dead hair. I think it's called shedding.

CHRISTMAS

I have been waiting for this Holiday for a whole month and Dad cannot seem to get out of bed. He's complaining about a headache and upset stomach because of all he ate and drank last night.

Honestly, I don't care, and all I can think about is the Christmas stocking hanging in front of the fireplace with new toys inside for me. I was told not to think about trying to get these toys; so I am forced to wait for someone to go downstairs.

There is hope. Mom is getting out of bed to take me for a piddle. This could be my chance. Mom seems to have some other things on her mind. She's not interested in me; she's not going back to sleep and she's not even taking off her coat...

Wait Mom, it's Christmas, you know, and I've been a good dog; I come when you call, I wait to be fed, I try not to jump on you and Dad and I sleep through the night without bothering you. Where are you going?

She's back. I'm really anxious now. Will she remember? Will Dad remember? How could either of them eat breakfast and forget about me? I'm just going to have to be obnoxious and pester them...

Let's see, how about a little nudge, a little barking and a little pointing in the direction of the fireplace ... no luck ... nothing yet. They just don't understand! I will have to resort to jumping up at the table and really get annoying with a squeak toy.

Wait. . . I think the squeak toy is working. Mom is finally getting up, but she's heading for the camera... Mom, do you really have to take pictures right now? She's leading me to the living room...

I can hardly wait. I hope she isn't going to spend all day taking pictures of me in front of the fireplace looking at my stocking and all my unopened toys. Oh boy, she's putting the camera down and now she's moving over to my stocking. I am so excited...

She's reaching into the stocking and she's holding a new toy for me. It's great! It's a snowman squeak toy just like the one I asked for from Santa. How did she know?

Santa must have called her from the North Pole. It looks like there is more in my stocking besides the snowman. Boy am I lucky that Mom and Dad didn't forget *Good Boy Jesse*. How could they forget me?

I must be making Christmas worthwhile for them, too. I am giving them the spirit of the season without the cost of a college education. I am filling their lives with total love and devotion for the cost of a few squeak toys and some bones. I am licking their faces and giving them attention. Isn't that what Christmas is all about?

I hope I don't have to wait a whole year for more new toys. I will be very good and make sure that Mom and Dad never forget their favorite and only child, *Good Boy Jesse*.

HO HO HO!

Me playing in the snow

HAPPINESS IS...

When I think about being happy, I think about how I feel when Mom and Dad are around. There is a good feeling in my heart that makes me want to play and act like a puppy again.

I absolutely love to chase Dad around the kitchen after supper. He grabs one of my toys and we play hide and seek around the kitchen wall. I chase him and then he chases me. It is so much fun and I know Dad has a great time because he and Mom are always laughing when we play this game. Another thing I do when I'm happy is to roll on my back on the rug in the bedroom. It feels so good! I can stretch my legs up in the air and wiggle back and forth with my head upside down.

Sometimes I feel so comfortable that I fall asleep in this position. I wake up and see Mom and Dad looking at me with that look that says, "We love you, Jesse, you are so adorable." I don't know how I do it, but I make them feel great, too! How do I know they feel great? A dog like me just knows!

I have what people call animal instinct. It's the knack of being lighthearted every minute of the day and making everyone happy around me. I don't know how to act any other way.

I have this natural ability to smile and the world smiles with me. I hold no grudges and forgive and forget in about five minutes. Life is too short. I make the best of every situation and just have a wonderful time wherever I go.

So, happiness is the state I am in all the time. As long as I have my sense of dog humor, what else matters? Mom and Dad love me just the way I am.

How do I know? They tell me all the time. If you ask me to summarize in one sentence, I would tell you that I am grateful for the life that I have and I am happy to be me, *Good Boy Jesse*.

It just doesn't get any better than this!

EPILOGUE: MOM SPEAKS

Dad is speechless. In fact, I had to walk him over to the sofa and let him lie down after I read Jesse's book to him.

He was in shock. Of course, I knew that Jesse was capable of super dog powers all the time. I have been telling Dad for months that I knew what Jesse was thinking, and was right on target.

I just put myself in his place. This is an animal that has everything. All the comforts of home and a doting Mom and Dad. What a life. We will have a line forming outside our front door with dogs of all breeds just waiting to be adopted when Jesse's book is published.

Well, Jesse, where did you come from? How did you know I was thinking about you right now? You must be tired from all that writing.

Come on, let's relax...

Jesse; you are quite a guy! You have brought laughter, life and love into our lives. You are the reason we get up in the morning and are happy to be alive. You are the all-forgiving, all-loving and all-adoring animal in all of us who simply wants to love and be loved.

You don't want to earn money, read great books, discover the cure for cancer or become the President of the United States.

You are not an actor or a rock star. You certainly cannot leap tall buildings or fly like an eagle. You will never be a doctor, a lawyer or an Indian Chief.

You will never be anything but a dog. Not such a bad deal, Jesse, not such a bad deal at all!

EPILOGUE: DAD SPEAKS

I cannot believe Jesse's book. I keep thinking about all the things he wrote and I never realized that he was capable of human thoughts.

Mom kept telling me he was smart, but this goes far beyond being smart. I also knew that Golden Retrievers were good natured and made good companions, but not to this extent.

I will take some of the credit for his behavior because of the way he was raised. I never allowed him to get away with anything. If he misbehaved, he was reprimanded and I reminded him that he was a "Bad Dog". That was my job as his Dad.

I never once let anything slide by, and even Jesse knew when I was about to give him one of my disappointed looks. His tail would go right between his legs and he would come right over to me and ask for forgiveness by putting his paw on my leg.

In his mind, he was always wrong and only wanted me to say that it was "OK" again. This discipline makes the difference between an ordinary dog and a *Good Boy Jesse*.

Mom has her own way of letting Jesse know who's boss and it's called motherly love. Jesse has been treated with special care since he was a puppy.

He has only listened to classical music and has indicated that he likes Mozart the best. He has a regular routine of meals, play, walks and grooming which is very satisfying to any dog's needs.

He also has Mom and Dad around the house for entertainment. What more could any dog ask for? Oh no, did I hear someone say something? Is that you, Jesse? What? Oh, you think that a little puppy to play with would be fun? Well, we'll have to see what Mom has to say...

TRIBUTE

Thank you, Mom and Dad, for taking me into your lives. I will always be there for you in good times and in bad times. You must know how much I love you. To live with a dog is the closest any human can get to being a dog.

From my own personal experience, being a dog is the best! I can't think of any other animal I would rather be. Without you, Mom and Dad, I'm just an ordinary dog. You're the ones that have made the difference. I've looked around, done some comparison shopping, and I know quality when I sniff it! So, please don't leave me alone too often and don't forget to buy me new toys.

Please don't go to sleep without a big hug for *Good Boy Jesse*. In return, I'll be your best friend and a good boy. You are everything to me. I am your greatest fan. We make quite a family, don't we?

Believe in me, Mom and Dad, and I will never let you down. If you only knew the wonderful feeling I have when we are all together, you would never doubt my devotion. Just look in my eyes and trust what you see; true love in the purest form.

Me and Mom out for a walk in the park

DREAMS

I picture myself as a very famous author. I am traveling all over the world with Mom and Dad. We are going to schools lecturing about the importance of dogs in the family. We are invited to appear on morning, afternoon and late night talk shows.

We are recognized wherever we go as the *Good Boy Jesse* family. It is wonderful. (Of course we are all wearing dark sunglasses, too!)

We remind people to appreciate what they have and to be lucky that they are alive. We spread the message of peace to all warring nations. We are like a cool breeze on a hot summer day... great!

Suddenly... I awake! I blink my eyes and look around and realize that I have been dreaming for a long time. What an incredible imagination for a dog! I will tell you one more time; I'm not just an ordinary dog, or am I? I think I'll let you be the judge...

As I end my book, I am certain that you will always have a warm place in your heart for *Good Boy Jesse*.

By the way, that low rumble in my throat that you may have heard from time to time means "I love you." It's the best way for me to communicate all my inner gratitude for the love and attention I get from my human friends.

I'll leave you here with a lick and a promise ...The lick is a big wet one right on your cheek, and the promise is that you will always look at any dog and know why they were put on this Earth. The answer is in their eyes and the low rumble in their throat.

Older and much wiser, with my white face

FROM THE AUTHOR

Jesse was my first and only dog. Remembering my life with this precious animal has triggered feelings of warmth, joy and love.

Being alone was never a problem, because Jesse kept me company.

Conversation was never dull when Jesse became the main subject.

We developed a form of conversation that elicited that low rumble in his throat and I imagined what he was saying in response to all my questions and complaints.

Watching other people with their dogs always reminds me of my journey with Jesse and I wonder what I would have done without him by my side. Sharing his story and closing the last chapter has made me smile. I am eternally grateful for the love of a dog named Jesse.

THE END

Jesse and Mom

Bilingual Editions of *Good Boy Jesse* Available Now

Italian-English & English-Italian

Spanish-English & English-Spanish

www.BestBilingual.com

CPSIA information can be obtained at www.ICGtesting.com
Printed in the USA
BVOW10s1210041213

338007BV00006BA/15/P

9 781619 954595